Amelia Earhart

Published in the United States of America by Cherry Lake Publishing
Ann Arbor, Michigan
www.cherrylakepublishing.com

Content Adviser: Ryan Emery Hughes, Doctoral Student, School of Education, University of Michigan
Reading Adviser: Marla Conn, ReadAbility, Inc.
Book Design: Jennifer Wahi
Illustrator: Jeff Bane

Photo Credits: © frank thompson photos/Flickr, 5; © B Christopher/Alamy, 7; © Pictorial Press Ltd/Alamy, 9; © Everett Historical/Shutterstock Images, 11, 13, 22, 23; © Everett Collection Historical Alamy, 15; © Harris & Ewing/Library of Congress, 17; © JMcic, 19; © AF archive/Alamy, 21; Cover, 8, 12, 18, Jeff Bane; Various frames throughout, Shutterstock Images

Library of Congress Cataloging-in-Publication Data

Haldy, Emma E., author.
  Amelia Earhart / Emma E. Haldy.
     pages cm. -- (My itty bitty bio)
  Audience: K to grade 3.
  Includes bibliographical references and index.
  ISBN 978-1-63470-480-9 (hardcover) -- ISBN 978-1-63470-540-0 (pdf) -- ISBN 978-1-63470-600-1 (pbk.) -- ISBN 978-1-63470-660-5 (ebook)
  1. Earhart, Amelia, 1897-1937--Juvenile literature. 2. Women air pilots--United States--Biography--Juvenile literature. 3. Air pilots--United States--Biography--Juvenile literature. I. Title.
  TL540.E3H35 2016
  629.13092--dc23
  [B]
                              2015026082

Printed in the United States of America
Corporate Graphics

About the author: Emma E. Haldy is a former librarian and a proud Michigander. She lives with her husband, Joe, and an ever-growing collection of books.

About the illustrator: Jeff Bane and his two business partners own a studio along the American River in Folsom, California, home of the 1849 Gold Rush. When Jeff's not sketching or illustrating for clients, he's either swimming or kayaking in the river to relax.

I was born in Kansas in 1897.

I was close to my grandparents.
I had one sister.

I was active. I was curious.

I played sports. I loved to read.

What are your favorite activities?

I went to college. I worked as a **social worker**.

One day, I discovered flying. I loved it. It was all I wanted to do with my life.

Some people said women should not fly. But I trained with **pilots**. I learned to fly.

I bought my own plane. I flew as much as I could.

I became the first woman to fly over the Atlantic Ocean.

I became very famous. I won awards. I met important people.

I married George Putnam.
He was my **publisher**.

He supported my **career**.
We were partners and friends.

I kept flying. I set more records.

I was the first person to fly alone over the Atlantic and Pacific Oceans.

What records would you like to break?

I decided to take one last big trip.

I wanted to circle the **globe**.

Something went wrong. No one could find me or my plane. I was never found.

I was a brave woman. I was a flying **pioneer**. I set an example for women.

What would you like to ask me?

1900

1921

Born
1897

Died
1937

1928

2000

glossary

career (kuh-REER) a person's work or jobs

globe (GLOHB) the world

pilots (PYE-luhts) people who fly airplanes

pioneer (pye-uh-NEER) one of the first people to work in a new field

publisher (PUHB-lish-ur) someone who makes and sells books and other reading materials

social worker (SOH-shuhl WUR-kur) someone who helps people with money or family problems

index